Qumran ar
Jewish Jesus

Reading the New Testament in the Light of the Scrolls

George J Brooke

Rylands Professor of Biblical Criticism and Exegesis,
University of Manchester

GROVE BOOKS LIMITED
RIDLEY HALL RD CAMBRIDGE CB3 9HU

Contents

The Cover Illustration is by Dona McCullagh

First Impression March 2005
ISSN 1365-490X
ISBN 1 85174 587 4

Caves, Codes, and Conspiracies 1

This booklet is intended to convince you that the manuscripts that have come out of eleven caves at Qumran on the northwest shore of the Dead Sea are very important for understanding various aspects of Judaism at the time of Jesus.

But let it be said from the outset that the Dead Sea Scrolls are not any part of some secret conspiracy. I have been working closely on the scrolls for over thirty years and know of no scholars or church leaders or anybody else who has any secret knowledge deriving from the scrolls which is being held back for some clandestine reason. Pictures of *all* the thousands of fragments have been available for over a decade, and nearly all of the fragments have been published in detailed editions, usually with English translations and notes; everything is accessible and nowadays it is available electronically too. Conspiracy theories will no doubt persist; it is, after all, impossible to refute them without being labelled as part of the conspiracy itself. Nevertheless, the information that comes from the scrolls is actually far more important and interesting than any such theory.

If not conspiracy, then how about mystery? The discovery of the Dead Sea Scrolls has sometimes been talked about as the greatest archaeological find of the twentieth century. The romance of such amazing

The information that comes from the scrolls is actually far more important and interesting than any conspiracy theory

discoveries, as with the opening of tombs and the uncovering of magnificent mummies in Egypt, provokes all kinds of response in the public imagination. Some items in the collection are indeed remarkable and surprising, such as the penmanship involved in the micro-writing on some fragments, or the occasional curious use of cryptic alphabets (all now decoded and published), or the Copper Scroll's list of buried treasure (probably all found by the Romans long ago). However, certain key matters cannot really be gainsaid:

- First, the scrolls from Qumran are all Jewish; there are no Christian scrolls (as Dan Brown, for one, mischievously claims in *The Da Vinci Code*).

- Second, at the time of his public ministry Jesus was definitely not an Essene; because of the particular stances he takes on many issues, almost certainly he never had been one, though we know so little about his early life.

- Third, the scrolls must be understood as providing us with all kinds of information about Judaism at the time of Jesus and not just the views of a small isolated minority who lived in the desert.

Put all three of those points together and it is immediately clear that the scrolls have much to teach us about Jewish life in Palestine at the time of Jesus. They provide a wealth of textual and other information for the proper reconstruction of Judaism in the two centuries before the Roman destruction of the temple in AD 70. For people interested in the Jewish Jesus and his early followers, they cannot be ignored as the primary source for providing many details of their historical context. At a time of constant historical scepticism about Jesus, they help show what kind of Jew Jesus was and they highlight what was distinctive about his teaching and way of life.

For people interested in the Jewish Jesus and his early followers, the scrolls cannot be ignored

General Orientation

2

The Dead Sea Scrolls

The term Dead Sea Scrolls is applied to a variety of manuscript finds from the general region of the Judaean Wilderness, to the west and north of the Dead Sea itself. Amongst the most well-known places where manuscripts have been discovered is Masada, the impregnable fortress which was most elaborately constructed by Herod the Great and then finally captured after a famous siege and largely destroyed by the Romans in AD 74, at the end of the first Jewish revolt (AD 66–74). All of these various manuscript finds date from after the Second World War, though the manuscripts themselves date from the fourth century BC to the eighth century AD. This booklet is entitled 'Qumran and the Jewish Jesus' because it is concerned solely with the manuscripts which were found in eleven caves at and near Qumran between 1947 and 1956.

Qumran

Qumran is the name given to the small settlement on a clay and limestone terrace above the northwest corner of the Dead Sea, some 8½ miles south of Jericho. In the Second Temple period, the site was occupied between c 100–75 BC and AD 68, with a short break towards the end of the reign of Herod the Great for reasons which are not entirely clear.

Most scholars are happy to say that those who inhabited the site were Essenes, a Jewish group in Palestine of about the same size and active at the same time as the Pharisees and Sadducees. The Essenes were of two types according to classical sources, the marrying and the non-marrying kind. Though widely regarded in antiquity as exemplary for their piety and simple way of life, it is important to realize that the Essenes cannot be neatly stereotyped. Like any relatively small denominational group, the Essenes were made up of diverse sub-groups and over the two hundred years of their history these differing segments of the movement seem to have gone through various changes and developments. Apart from the sectarian scrolls from the Qumran caves, the modern knowledge of the Essenes comes chiefly from three sources. In the

Most scholars are happy to say that those who inhabited the site were Essenes

writings of the Egyptian Jewish philosopher Philo, who was an earlier contemporary of Jesus, and in the works of Josephus the Jewish historian whose literary activity dates from the thirty years after the destruction of Jerusalem in AD 70, there are detailed descriptions of Essene beliefs and practices. Pliny the Elder, the Roman natural historian, wrote an important but brief paragraph on the Essenes who live west of the shore of the Dead Sea between Jericho and Ein Gedi; this is the most direct reference to the Qumran section of the Essenes and most obviously links some Essenes to the site where the scrolls were found.

The Scrolls from the Qumran Caves

The Qumran scrolls themselves are a collection of approximately nine hundred manuscripts. They are referred to either by cave number, the letter Q (=Qumran), and a short title, such as *Rule of the Community*, or by cave number, Q, and a number, such as 4Q252 (=*Commentary on Genesis* A). A superscript letter after the title indicates that the manuscript contains one of a series of extant copies of the same composition (*eg*, 4QS^e = the fifth copy of the *Rule of the Community* from Cave 4); a capital letter after the title indicates that the manuscript contains one of a series of compositions of a very similar genre. The manuscripts are dated on the basis of the styles of the hands in which they are written and through the application of Carbon 14 techniques to some of them. They were penned between the third century BC and the time that Qumran was destroyed in AD 68. From the kinds of scribal practices in the manuscripts, especially a range of spelling systems, it seems as if only a limited number of the scrolls may actually have been written at Qumran. The majority would have been brought there from Jerusalem and elsewhere.

The majority of the Qumran scrolls would have been brought there from Jerusalem and elsewhere

The 'Biblical' Manuscripts

The manuscripts are commonly divided into three groups. In the first can be put about two hundred copies of those books which ended up in the Jewish Bible and through a different route in the Christian Old Testament. The books of the Torah, especially Genesis and Deuteronomy, are well represented, as are some of the literary Prophets, notably Isaiah and the Twelve; and the Psalms are represented in three or more different editions. Several of the books which are assigned in Judaism to the Writings, the third part of the canon, are not so well represented, and though Ezra–Nehemiah, 1 and 2 Chronicles and Esther were all clearly known by the community, they are not represented in the collection apart from a few scraps. Other works, no longer considered universally authoritative, were so to the movement of which the Qumran community was a part, such as the *Book of Jubilees* (present in numerous copies in the Qumran caves and cited as an authority in the *Damascus Document*: CD 16.2–4).

The Sectarian Manuscripts

In the second group are about two hundred manuscripts which contain compositions which can be clearly labelled as sectarian. These describe the organization and beliefs of some of the various communities which made up the Essene movement. Some of the compositions, such as the *Rule of the Congregation* (1QSa), even describe the movement's ideal configuration at the end of time (in which, for example, women and children play a full part), part of which may have been anticipated in some sections of the community's present. In this sub-group of scrolls can be put the very few documentary texts which survive; perhaps the written business dealings of parts of the Qumran community were stored elsewhere than in the caves. Items from this collection of sectarian manuscripts have often been compared with matters in the New Testament. The similarities struck scholars right from the beginning. For example, the communal sharing of goods seems to have been practised in some form by the Essenes, perhaps in terms of the community being able to benefit from any member's capital, though its ownership probably remained with the individual member; this has often been compared with the depiction in Acts 4.32–5.11 of shared property. Or again, it is in these sectarian compositions that particular offices are mentioned, such as the *mebaqqer*, 'inspector,' 'examiner,' or 'overseer,' a position likened to that of the *episkopos*, 'bishop' or 'overseer,' in the pastoral letters (1 Timothy 3.1–7). Nowadays, it is often the differences between the Essene and early Christian uses of similar motifs that is commented upon.

Items from this collection of sectarian manuscripts have often been compared with matters in the New Testament

The Remaining Manuscripts

In the third group are the remaining manuscripts. These contain literary compositions, some of which were known before, such as some of the books associated with Enoch (an item which was preserved by Christian groups and which seems to have been authoritative for the author of Jude; see Jude 14–15), but most of which had been lost to the reading public for nearly two thousand years. Some features of this non-biblical, non-sectarian collection are worth noting. To begin with, it is clear that this is a Jewish collection; there are virtually no traces of any literature from the Gentile world—there is no Greek philosophy or drama, no Latin literature. However, this does not mean that there are no Hellenistic influences in the compositions; it is apparent,

7

It is clear that this is a Jewish collection; there are virtually no traces of any literature from the Gentile world

for example, that some of the calendrical and astrological compositions are entirely current with the latest scientific knowledge. Furthermore, although this third group might best be described as consisting of general Jewish literature from the period, some Jewish compositions are strikingly absent—there is nothing of the Maccabean literature, nor of early Jewish literature which we know was composed in Greek, such as the Wisdom of Solomon.

Despite the way in which the contents of the manuscripts can be viewed as being somewhat repetitive and restricted through the way they share many ideas, this library extends our knowledge of general Jewish literature enormously. The full publication of nearly all the fragmentary manuscripts since 1991 has enabled major advances in respect of all three categories of literature:

- For the 'biblical' manuscripts we can learn about the immensely complex history of the transmission of the constituent parts of the Old Testament. These scrolls indicate that the medieval rabbinic texts from which all Protestant and most Roman Catholic Old Testaments are translated preserve authentic texts from antiquity, but that they were not the only or in every case even the oldest form of the text in circulation at the time of Jesus.

- From the sectarian compositions we can learn about community pluralism. There is not just one static group called the Essenes, but several strands of Essenism coexisting at the same time and each with its own complex organizational development and history.

- From the remaining compositions we can learn much that contributes not least to the better contextualization within Palestinian Judaism of the life and teaching of Jesus and his first followers.

The Qumran Caves

Before moving to the closer description and analysis of the scrolls from the Qumran caves, it is important to say a few words about the manuscripts in the collection in relation to the caves where they were discovered. A common supposition is that the manuscripts were all put in the caves to hide them from the Romans who came to attack

A common supposition is that the manuscripts were all put in the caves to hide them from the Romans who came to attack

the site in AD 68 as they were on their way down the Jordan valley before turning west towards Jerusalem to quell the Jewish revolt. Though it is possible that a few of the manuscripts were indeed deposited in one or two of the caves for such a reason, the matter is more complicated.

To begin with, the caves are of two sorts. On the one hand there are natural caves in the hillsides above the Qumran site. There are hundreds of these caves formed through the movement of the valley at times of earthquake. Many of these caves show signs of habitation from the Hellenistic and Roman periods. Only three of the manuscript caves are of this type, Caves 1, 3, and 11. On the other hand there are the man-made caves in the clay and limestone terraces on which the community buildings are situated or near to it.

It is indeed likely that Cave 1 is best understood as a genizah, a burial place for manuscripts no longer in use

The manuscripts in Cave 1 were discovered wrapped in linen and carefully placed in jars. It was as if they had been buried and it is indeed likely that the Cave is best understood as a *genizah*, a burial place for manuscripts, which reflects customary Jewish practice for manuscripts no longer in use. In other words, those manuscripts in Cave 1, which include for us some of the best preserved, were probably the most damaged in antiquity and had been deposited, probably well before the end of the first century BC, because they could no longer be used. Nearly six hundred very fragmentary manuscripts have been recovered from Cave 4, which is very close to the Qumran site. This Cave is naturally air-conditioned by the desert winds which come up the valley and seems to have formed some kind of working repository. In Cave 8 were found a large number of tabs for strengthening the edges of manuscripts and ties for holding them closed when they were rolled up; it seems likely that this cave served as a workshop where some manuscripts were finished off with the necessary items, though it could have been merely a store for such things.

It seems likely that Cave 8 served as a workshop where some manuscripts were finished off with strengthening tabs and ties

Cave 7 can only be accessed by going through the community's buildings; it is at the end of the terrace on which they are built. From this cave have come only a few manuscript fragments, but they are all in Greek. Although some scholars, such as C P Thiede, have been determined to argue that some of the fragments are parts of some of the writings now to be found in the New Testament, this is highly unlikely. For example, one fragment is supposed by this small group of scholars to be part of the Gospel of Mark, but only one word can be read securely ('and') and to fit the text of Mark to the few other extant letters requires adjusting the text of Mark in ways for which there is no other supporting textual evidence. Several of those fragments which have been thought to belong to parts of the New Testament are much better understood as part of the writings of Enoch in Greek. This is fascinating in itself, because it seems likely that some members of the Qumran community could read or even speak Greek, as well as Hebrew and Aramaic; perhaps some members had Greek as their first language.

Having set out some background issues in relation to the scrolls, we now need to explore what the relationship might be, if any, between the scrolls themselves and the documents of the New Testament. Out of this we can then draw some implications for the impact our knowledge of the scrolls will have on our actual reading of the New Testament itself.

Close Encounters?

3

Bazaar Theories

How should the scrolls from the eleven Qumran caves and the writings of the New Testament be related? One of the main aims of this booklet is to argue that the two bodies of literature cannot be related directly. It is very unlikely that Jesus or any of the New Testament authors had ever read any of the scrolls discovered in those caves, though they may well have been familiar

It is very unlikely that Jesus or any of the New Testament authors had ever read any of the scrolls discovered in those caves

with some of the compositions found in them. In other words it is probably the case that the best way to view the scrolls is to appreciate that they provide the literary context for reconstructing a large amount of our knowledge of Judaism in Palestine at the time of Jesus. In fact, it is now seldom recalled that before the Dead Sea Scrolls were discovered, all that there was in Hebrew and Aramaic from the regions of Judaea and Galilee from the time of Jesus were a few coin inscriptions and some names inscribed on ossuaries, those bone boxes which became fashionable in Jerusalem in the first century BC for secondary burials. The scrolls, especially those from Qumran, have given us the remains of several hundred compositions in Hebrew and Aramaic, as well as a few in Greek, which not only fill out the picture of the richness and variety of Judaism at the turn of the eras, but also change the modern reconstruction of Jewish life and practice at the time of Jesus in many significant ways. This kind of sober perspective on the relationship between the scrolls and the New Testament does not make for eye-catching headlines. Rather, it is concerned to use the scrolls to contextualize the teaching of Jesus and the writings of the New Testament.

This kind of sober perspective does not make for eye-catching headlines

But there have long been and continue to be other ways of relating the scrolls and the New Testament. There has always been a significant group of scholars who have distanced the scrolls from Jesus and the writings of the first Christians. There are various good reasons for taking this line, though some of these have been undermined somewhat in recent years. There is indeed the need to recall that the scrolls found at Qumran are largely a collection belonging to an educated priestly elite, many of whom would have been most at home in Jerusalem and its environs and whose major concern was for a stringent ritual purity. By contrast, Jesus and his first followers are northerners and from agricultural and artisan backgrounds. It is often noted how striking it is that the gospels mention neither Sepphoris nor Tiberias, the major cities of the area in which Jesus taught; the implication is that he did not make those significant towns a focus of his ministry. Furthermore Jesus' teaching is dominated with agricultural motifs and his daily company and social interactions included many who would have been widely considered by their fellow Jews as outside the community of Jewish worship, whether in a synagogue or occasionally at the Jerusalem temple.

However, whilst the differences can be suitably used to stress that Jesus was not an Essene, they should not be allowed to obscure the way in which there are several common issues and concerns which are particularly illuminated from a consideration of the scrolls. In particular any doctrinaire approach which tries to protect the uniqueness of the language used about Jesus from historical investigation is to be seen as merely putting one's head in the sand. For example, the titles 'Son of God' and 'Son of the Most High' occur together in 4Q246, an Aramaic non-sectarian composition which predates Luke 1.32–35 by at least two centuries. It is highly likely that Luke's usage of the same combination of titles should be understood in light of the messianic statements of 4Q246.

The real money in the book bazaar, however, is to be made by those who construct bizarre theories about the close relationship between the Qumran scrolls, Jesus and the New Testament which assert their proximity, and not just their proximity but that John the Baptist, Jesus and their followers grew out of the movement which we now know from Qumran. These theories take several different shapes, but most of them share some common features. For a start, it is common amongst those who write in this vein to criticize or ridicule the ways in which the manuscripts from Qumran have been dated. This is because many of the theories depend upon reading some of the sectarian scrolls as if they speak of John the Baptist or some other early Christian character such as James or Paul. However, it needs to be stated clearly that though the palaeographic and carbon datings cannot be entirely precise, it seems as if the vast amount of manuscripts come from the first century

Even if a few of the manuscripts date from the first century AD, the composition on any such manuscript is likely to be considerably earlier

BC and so are pre-Christian. Furthermore, even if a few of the manuscripts are from the first century AD, none is apparently an autograph (that is, the original manuscript), so the composition on any such manuscript is likely to be considerably earlier. Another general characteristic of these theories is their insistence that things that look similar must be the same. Thus, such theories generally only describe the similarities between the data they juxtapose; they tend to ignore the many differences.

In recent years those who have published money-making books have generally avoided claiming that Jesus himself was a fully-fledged Essene. John the Baptist may well have known about the Essenes, and even the Essenes of Qumran, though his apparent individualism makes it very unlikely that he was ever a member. It is particularly unlikely that he was the Teacher of Righteousness (the founding figure of the movement referred to in several sectarian scrolls), as some, such as Barbara Thiering, have claimed. It cannot be denied that both in the scrolls and in the New Testament the rite of admission to the various communities is described in terms of ritual washing and the presence of the Holy Spirit (*Rule of the Community* [1QS] 3.6–9; Acts 19.1–7). However, it should not be assumed that such similarities must be explained by making them refer to the same thing. It should be noted that the early Christians tried to differentiate between John's baptism and that of their own practice (as Acts 19 implies). In a similar way, there could well be distance between the kind of baptism for repentance associated by the gospel writers with John and the kind of initiation rite practised by the Essenes. For the Essenes such initiation was just the start of a journey of ongoing ritual purification.

For the Essenes such initiation was just the start of a journey of ongoing ritual purification

As for Jesus, because of his very different attitudes to purity and his open-ended table fellowship, it is clear from the gospels that he was not a card-carrying member of the movement. Because of this, some modern authors have been tempted to say that Jesus had once been a member of the Essene movement but that for reasons of his own he had come to reject their rigidity and had become a renegade. This is pure speculation, by Thiering and others, that runs away with the enormous gift of the scrolls for a suitable historical reconstruction of much of the Judaism of Jesus' day and forces Jesus into a particular mould.

Another version of the theory that Jesus was close to Essenism in some way and that has also sold very well is put over by R H Eisenman. He has argued that the gospels present a picture of Jesus especially softened for Gentile readers. He stresses the few hints of a more militant Jesus still preserved in the gospels (such as Matthew 10.34) to suggest that the nationalistic, xenophobic kind

Eisenman glosses over the differences between the many groups he describes

of Judaism represented in some of the sectarian scrolls was preserved by Jesus and members of his family, especially James, over against the innovative Paul who adapted the militancy to put over a message that would permit Christians to fit in with the mores of the general Hellenistic culture of the Roman Mediterranean. But Eisenman glosses over the differences between the many groups he describes and at least part of his theory, identifying James as the Teacher of Righteousness, is based on a very unlikely redating of the manuscripts from Qumran.

The many similarities between the scrolls and the New Testament show that the scrolls should not be dismissed as irrelevant for understanding Jesus and his earliest followers. The many differences between the scrolls and the New Testament show that neither John the Baptist nor Jesus can be portrayed as the direct heirs of the kind of Judaism to be found in the sectarian scrolls. The similarities and the differences together indicate that the relationship between these two bodies of more or less contemporary literature is far more complicated. A more nuanced and sober perspective on the relationship between the scrolls and the New Testament that does not necessarily make for lucrative book contracts is required.

Were They All In Sects?

For centuries much of the presentation of Judaism in Palestine in the decades around the turn of the era has been based on the writings of the Jewish historian Josephus. Alongside a copy of the Bible, many 18th and 19th century households in Britain possessed an edition of William Whiston's 1737 rendering of Josephus. Josephus' influence on modern historiography is still very great, though it has been corrected suitably in many ways. For our purposes it is important to note that Josephus provides for his largely Gentile readership a model of the elites of Judaism which is enduring. For him there were three philosophies which he calls *haeresis*, 'sects': Pharisees, Sadducees, and Essenes. Later on there was also a fourth philosophy, the Zealots. When understood visually, it is as if the most convenient way of viewing Palestinian Judaism of the two centuries before the fall of the temple in AD 70 is as groups occupying discrete spaces, with little in common with each other. To some extent a superficial reading of the gospels seemed to confirm this as the Pharisees and Sadducees variously appear on the scene.

All this has tended to result in a depiction of Judaism as made up of a collection of groups; each group is seen as distinct in its views and also as coherent and somewhat monolithic in its own organization. Part of the problem in locating Jesus and his first followers arises from accepting Josephus's portrayal too quickly. The question is posed: 'Which group is Jesus most like?' And the answers come back in a variety of ways. As we have seen, the most financially rewarding viewpoint has been to assert that Jesus and his followers were the heirs of Essenism in some way. The more common view recently has been that Jesus seems to have shared most with the Pharisees, the party with whom he is portrayed as being in constant dialogue. But is this picture of Judaism as led by highly distinct, well-organized, and static groups correct?

Two groups of manuscripts have tended to undermine this view. First, the so-called *Halakhic Letter* (*Miqṣat Ma'aśe ha-Torah*=MMT) shows that the immediate predecessors of the Qumran community at the end of the second century BC tried to convince outsiders of the value of their position, arguing on the basis of Scripture and tradition. The text is a kind of circular which speaks of a 'we' group and a 'you' group. It is probably addressed to non-Essenes and indicates that the movement was not entirely cut off from other Jews. It is important to note some items in the content of MMT because these underline what the writer had in common with other Jews. In putting over a particular perspective on the interpretation of the Law, MMT affirms the importance of ritual purity, the significance of Jerusalem and the temple, and the place of the Law and the Prophets (and possibly some other authoritative texts). Noticing the common bases between various groups of Jews makes it less easy to discern quite where the boundaries between them should be drawn. As a result it is less easy to link Jesus and his followers clearly with one group rather than another, but it is appropriate to note that Jesus seems to have had views on all the same issues too—but that does not make him an Essene.

Second, the publication of the Cave 4 copies of the *Rule of the Community* has made clear that over the century or more that the *Rule* was variously copied out, subtle changes were introduced to reflect the changing patterns of organization in the movement, or, at least, in the part of it which the *Rule of the Community* represents. The Qumran community and the wider movement of which it was a part was not a static organization, but constantly changing. Most explicitly, whereas the Cave 1 copy of the *Rule* (1QS; *c* 100–75 BC) describes authority as vested in the

The Qumran community and the wider movement of which it was a part was not a static organization

sons of Zadok, the priests, in 4QS^d (*c* 30–1 BC) the same passage is constructed so that authority rests with the majority of the community ('the Many'). This implies that a group which may have already become institutionalized and hierarchical as it moved to Qumran at the beginning of the first century BC, somewhat later went through a process of rediscovering the equal authority of all its full members. It now seems that rather than thinking that the elite groups in Judaism had a fixed institutional stability, it should be recognized that even these groups constantly underwent changes, some of which were akin to charismatic renewal. As a result of this situation of organizational flux, when making any kinds of comparison it is necessary to ask with what stage of the Qumran community's development a feature of Jesus' life and practice or that of his followers is being juxtaposed.

These two points illuminate some matters in the New Testament. It is more appropriate to assume that Jesus and his early followers had more in common with other groups of Jews than that they were entirely innovative and distinct. Furthermore, the Jesus group and the communities of early Christians also went through many changes. From charismatic beginnings at the time of Jesus the early churches became increasingly hierarchical and formally organized, as in the Pastoral Epistles, though some of them, such as some of the communities reflected in the Johannine literature, went through the rediscovery of egalitarian first principles. Jewish sectarianism at the time of Jesus is not as clear-cut as it may at first glance have seemed.

Jewish sectarianism at the time of Jesus is not as clear-cut as it may at first glance have seemed

The Jubilees Line

Although it is important to talk about what all Jews had in common and to underline that all groups were more dynamic than static, nevertheless it is also obvious that the various Jewish groups at the time of Jesus did have some distinctive views. The sectarian compositions from Qumran indicate that one of the most significant disputes in Judaism at the time of Jesus and probably for some centuries before then concerned the calendar. The Qumran community and the wider movement of which it was a part had a particular take on the calendar and also on how the periods of history should be calculated.

For the calendar it is now known from the various Qumran calendar compositions that those at Qumran gave particular priority to the seven-day week as the basis of their view of how God had organized sacred time. From their knowledge of actual astronomical observations they tried to integrate the lunar cycle of approximately four weeks with their view of the perfect year as consisting of 364 days (exactly 52 seven-day weeks). They did not simply follow a solar calendar, though they tended to subsume lunar calculations to solar ones. They did not invent this calendar. It is certainly present in the *Book of Jubilees* (middle of the 2nd century BC) and in the *Astronomical Treatise* in the writings associated with Enoch, which may be somewhat earlier. But it could be read out of Genesis itself: Noah was seen to have been in the ark for

364 days, from the seventeenth day of the second month (Genesis 7.11) to the twenty-seventh of the second month (Genesis 8.14), a year of 52 weeks.

For the periods of history the number seven was also the key. The line taken by the *Book of Jubilees* is that history runs in jubilee periods of forty-nine years each. For the author of the *Book of Jubilees* in his retelling of events in Genesis and the first part of Exodus the entry of the Israelites into the land takes place precisely at the end of the fiftieth jubilee after creation. Without the same precision in counting years, the author of the *Apocalypse of Weeks* in the writings associated with Enoch breaks history into ten weeks, while in the Enochic *Book of Watchers* (early 2nd century BC) there is apparently a scheme of eleven weeks. In the Damascus Document the exile is deemed to have lasted for 390 years; then after a further twenty years the Teacher arose to establish the community; after his death the author comments that there will be forty more years before God comes in judgment—perhaps all this fits into a scheme of 490 years from the exile until the end, if the Teacher is given a biblically rounded forty year ministry.

In Jerusalem the calendar in the Temple was apparently based on the lunar months with appropriate intercalations to bring the lunar calendar into line with the true solar year. Although all Jews would have shared the observance of the Sabbath on the same day each week, those guided by the Temple in Jerusalem would have observed festivals at different times from those who calculated things in some way like the members of the Qumran community. The inability for all Jews to celebrate the Jewish festivals together clearly marked one group off from another. Varieties of calendrical calculations may lie behind the differences in the dating of the crucifixion in relation to Passover between the author of John's gospel and those of the first three gospels.

The inability for all Jews to celebrate the Jewish festivals together clearly marked one group off from another

The reading of history in periods is most readily visible in the New Testament in the genealogies of Jesus. In particular in Luke 3.23–38 the genealogy has seventy-seven generations which pattern seems to echo the eleven weeks of the *Book of Watchers*. Perhaps Luke sourced his genealogy from a group of Christians who shared the same principles for calculating the periods of history as those who wrote the *Book of Watchers* or who preserved it at Qumran. Whatever the case, views about chronology and practices determined by a particular view of the calendar did indeed mark one Jewish group off from another.

The Gender Agenda

Another matter that is commonly thought to be a hallmark of the distinctiveness of the Qumran community is celibacy; it is sometimes even suggested that the Essenes as a whole were a celibate group with not a little misogyny in their overall outlook. The *Rule of the Community* has been read as confirmation of this. It contains not a mention of any women, except in once using the epithet 'born of a woman.' Pliny's description of the community at what may be the Qumran site as 'without women' has been held to support such a view, as also the descriptions of Philo (*Hypothetica* 14–17) and Josephus (*War* 2.120–21), though Josephus knows of a branch of the Essenes which permitted marriage (*War* 2.160–61). The presence of a few women's skeletons amongst the relatively small number of graves excavated in the main cemetery has yet to be fully explained in light of this opinion.

In fact, the situation in both the non-sectarian and the sectarian compositions from Qumran is more complicated. Amongst a range of data which puts the position of women in the movement in a different light three matters are particularly instructive in relation to the gospels. To begin with in the pre-sectarian wisdom text known as *Instruction* (4Q415), there is a small section which is addressed to a woman; its Hebrew verbal and pronominal suffixes are in the feminine. Even if this was supposed to be learnt by heart by men attending the wisdom school so that they could address it to their wives when they went home, the fragmentary paragraph still suggests that in the third or second century BC some Jewish women were receiving instruction in some matters, particularly pertaining to behaviour within marriage. This idea is confirmed in the sectarian *Rule of the Congregation* (1QSa), a rule for the community at the end of days, in which women and children are included amongst those who will be instructed in the precepts of the covenant. If the rule was in any way anticipated in the daily practices of the Qumran community or the wider movement of which it was a part, then perhaps women were already receiving instruction within Essenism. In the New Testament and even in the ministry of Jesus there are several examples of the inclusion of women at moments of instruction.

> *Women and children are included amongst those who will be instructed in the precepts of the covenant*

A second matter is explicit in one of the Cave 4 copies of the *Damascus Document*. Although no sectarian text has any member refer to another as 'brother' (or 'sister'), in 4QD[e] (4Q270) there is a rule which reads: 'One who murmurs against the fathers shall be expelled from the congregation and not return; if it is against the mothers, he shall be penalized for ten days, since the mothers do not wear a woven item indicating authority in the congregation.' Note first that some group labelled as 'mothers' seems to have some kind of responsibility within the congregation. Jesus' adaptation of familial terms as reported in a text like Mark 3.31–35 to create a new group based on fictive kinship may reflect a similar move. Whether the 'mothers' of the *Damascus Document* were ever at Qumran will never be known. Second, it is interesting that the difficult Hebrew of this passage in the *Damascus Document* links authority with some kind of garment; if Paul was aware of this practice amongst some Jews, then his insistence that at Corinth women should be veiled may be his way of enhancing the authority of the women there, as some scholars have argued on other grounds.

Third, it is surprising that in the *Rule of the Congregation* (1QSa; the ideal rule for the end of days which may have been anticipated in some community practices) there is indication that a woman may testify against her husband. It is likely that this concerns some kind of sexual misconduct since the *Damascus Document* states that a man can indeed be

> *It is intriguing to find in this supposedly misogynistic group that a woman's testimony was sometimes acceptable*

punished for committing fornication with his wife. Almost certainly this refers to prohibited sexual relations, perhaps during menstruation or pregnancy when there was no chance of procreation. Whatever the case, it is intriguing to find in this supposedly misogynistic group that a woman's testimony was sometimes acceptable. When this information is set alongside the resurrection accounts in the New Testament, notably Luke 24.10–12, it is apparent that the veracity of women's testimony was a live issue.

In these three intriguing examples can be seen material that compromises an oversimplified reading of the Qumran group or the Essene movement as having very peculiar attitudes to women. Instead, these three passages provide precisely the kind of information that helps to fill out our knowledge of Judaism at the time of Jesus so that some items in the New Testament are all the more intelligible to the modern reader.

4 Contexts and Connexions

Exegetical Exigencies

As has just been indicated the sectarian scrolls and the New Testament writings do indeed contain some intriguing similarities. Long ago scholars pointed out that some of the groups of each movement were organized along similar lines and had some very similar ideas for expressing their views of themselves, such as the use of the label 'the Way' (eg, 1QS 8.21, 'the way of perfection'; Acts 9.2, 'who belonged to the Way'). The complete publication of the manuscripts from Caves 4 and 11, which in some cases had remained on scholars' desks for nearly four decades, has shown that there are immense riches yet to be mined for the better understanding of all kinds of topics in both literary *corpora*. I consider that the most fruitful field of investigation will be concerned with the tracing of shared exegetical traditions, common issues in the interpretation of authoritative texts. In several instances we now have some striking overlaps in the handling of authoritative texts which show that the writers of some of the compositions now found in the Qumran library and the authors of the New Testament were the heirs of a common set of interpretative insights. In discussing such matters I consider that it is important not to be searching for closely defined lines of literary dependence, but for patterns of how the Scriptures could be read in early Palestinian Judaism. A few examples might whet the appetite.

The most fruitful field of investigation will be concerned with the tracing of shared exegetical traditions

In a non-sectarian composition, now officially known as the *Messianic Apocalypse* (4Q521), there is a description of some of the activities of a messiah. It seems as if the text depicts the realization of an ideal time through associating him with divine activity. Something has to be said about how in the whole of Jewish literature between the Bible and the Mishnah (c AD 200), it is only in 4Q521 and the Jesus saying in the double tradition of Luke and Matthew that Isaiah 61.1–2 is expanded with a statement about the raising of the dead. 'He will heal the wounded, and revive the dead and bring good news to the poor' says 4Q521; 'the dead are raised, the poor have good news brought to them' echoes Luke 7.22 as Jesus answers the disciples of John the Baptist concerning

> *The similarities in the exegetical handling of Isaiah and its expansion are too great to be brushed aside*

himself. Whether we conclude that Jesus must have known of this tradition directly from a Qumran source or that it was mediated to him some other way, the details of the similarities in the exegetical handling of Isaiah and its expansion are too great to be brushed aside.

Again, in a non-sectarian composition known as *Pseudo-Ezekiel*[a] (4Q385) in a description of the heavenly throne chariot there is a striking combination of some phrases of Ezekiel 1 with others from Ezekiel 10 and Isaiah 6. The same kind of interweaving of scriptural elements can be found in Revelation 4. Perhaps it is no surprise that in the descriptions of the throne chariot the parallel passages of Ezekiel 1 and 10 should be used, but the fact that both *Pseudo-Ezekiel* and Revelation also incorporate some clarificatory phrasing from Isaiah 6 suggests that both passages are the heirs of a common exegetical tradition in which Ezekiel and Isaiah were harmonized together to produce as full an authoritative picture of the divine throne as was possible on the basis of the Scriptures.

In a Greek manuscript of Leviticus found in Cave 4 (4Q119=4QLXXLev[a]) the text of Leviticus 26.9 seems to reflect something of the phrasing of Ezekiel 37.26 about the presence of the covenant amongst the people. In a similar way the reworked passages of Scripture that are to be found in the *Temple Scroll* (11Q19) 29.7–8 seem to combine Leviticus 26.12 with Ezekiel 37.23: 'they shall be for me a people and I will be for them for ever and I shall establish them for ever and always.' This editorial section of the *Temple Scroll*, like 4Q119, seems to give a good example of the intertextual relationship between Leviticus 26 and Ezekiel 37. This same relationship features in 2 Corinthians 6.14–7.1 which has often been compared with material in the scrolls; in this instance it only has to be noted that the text contains a string of quotations from Scripture beginning with Leviticus 26.12 and Ezekiel 37.27. There is no need to suggest that the writer of 2 Corinthians is dependent upon the Qumran texts for his material. Rather, all of the texts mentioned seem to be the heirs to a common interpretative tradition in which Leviticus 26 and Ezekiel 37 are read as mutually illuminating.

In sum, there is no direct literary dependence of the New Testament on the Qumran scrolls, but there are many shared ways of handling Scripture.

> *There is no direct literary dependence of the NT on the Qumran scrolls, but there are many shared ways of handling Scripture*

The Messianic Blanket

The scrolls from the eleven caves at and near Qumran also illuminate the ways in which Jesus is portrayed as messiah in the New Testament. The Qumran group and the movement of which it was a part were a priestly elite who were disenfranchised for most or all of their existence. Nobody likes being out of power for successive generations, but it seems as if many in the Qumran group took comfort from the development of views about the coming of God's agents who would vindicate them.

In the sectarian compositions there seem to be three figures who were looked for as the end seemed to be drawing near. There were two messiahs, a priestly one and a princely one, together with a prophet (as in 1QS 9.11). All three were thought of as anointed (which is what the term 'messiah' indicates); all three were of earthly human origin. The priestly messiah, sometimes called the 'Messiah of Aaron' always takes precedence over the princely one, sometimes called the 'Messiah of Israel.' In the somewhat later compositions (such as 4Q174) which speak of the messiahs, or at least one of them, the princely messiah is sometimes explicitly labelled as the 'Shoot of David,' picking up the language of Jeremiah 23.5. Perhaps this explicit Davidic messianism illustrates changing political aspirations in the community. The yearning for a particular figure to pick up the Davidic mantle may have been a deliberate attempt to assert traditional Israelite or Jewish views over against the non-Jewish rulers presiding over Judah and elsewhere from the time of Herod the Great onwards. The expected prophet is sometimes identified as Elijah returned (4Q558).

In the gospels the use of messianic labels is somewhat similar to that in the Qumran sectarian compositions

In the gospels the use of messianic labels is somewhat similar to that in the Qumran sectarian compositions. Though Jesus is portrayed as wishing to deny his followers the simple comfort of identifying him as a political conqueror about to oust the Romans, nevertheless the gospel writers show that some aspects of the standard views of the messiah in Judaism illuminate Jesus' role. Most often he is put alongside the traditions of Davidic messianism. Matthew is particularly keen on this aspect (Matthew 1.1), while John attempts to redefine the kind of kingly figure Jesus may be, especially as Jesus debates with Pilate (John 18.33–38). Matthew is also the most explicit of all the gospel writers in identifying John the Baptist as Elijah (Matthew 11.14), whereas both Luke and John prefer to reserve the role of prophet for Jesus as well; in John, John the Baptist explicitly denies he is the expected prophet (John 1.21). In John too there are a few features that hint that he likened Jesus to a priest; the note that his tunic was seamless (John 19.24) may be a reference to the high priest's robe.

The scrolls illustrate the range of ideas that can be associated with the roles of messianic figures. Their authors clearly expected separate figures to fulfil those roles. In the New Testament something of a similar range can be observed, but there, apart from Matthew's note about John the Baptist as Elijah, all the various roles are applied to Jesus, sometimes somewhat against his wishes. In light of the possible political role that Qumran's Davidic messiah was expected to play, it is likely that the Davidic designations applied to Jesus were intended to show that he was God's agent in bringing about God's rule. With the Qumran texts in mind the various New Testament applications of messianic titles can be seen as another take on Jewish aspirations of the time, rather than as something uniquely Christian.

Apart from Matthew's note about John the Baptist as Elijah, all the various roles are applied to Jesus

Riddled with Wisdom

Further examples of how the Qumran scrolls can illuminate the traditions present in the New Testament are to be found in the wide range of non-sectarian wisdom compositions. These enable us to reconsider the importance of wisdom traditions for understanding some aspects of the teaching of Jesus. Three brief examples can be given to suggest that those scholars who characterize Jesus' parabolic and other teaching as that of a wisdom teacher are indeed looking in the right direction.

Perhaps the most striking parallel to the teaching of Jesus is to be found in the so-called *Beatitudes* text (4Q525). The composition actually contains much wisdom teaching in addition to the beatitudes, but the beatitudes are part of the best-preserved part of the scroll (which is cited here with the line numbers of the fragment in parentheses and the spaces between the 'verses' indicated).

> [Blessed is the man who speaks the truth (?)] (1) with a pure heart,
>   and does not slander with his tongue. (space)
> Blessed are those who hold fast to her statutes,
>   and do not take hold of (2) the ways of iniquity. (space)
> Blessed are those who rejoice in her,
>   and do not utter in the ways of foolishness. (space)
> Blessed are those who seek her (3) with pure hands,
>   and do not search for her with a deceitful heart. (space)

> Blessed is the man who has attained Wisdom. (space)
>   He walks (4) in the Law of the Most High,
>   and prepares his heart for her ways. (space)
> And he controls himself by her instructions,
>   and always takes pleasure in her corrections,
>   (5) and does not forsake her in the afflictions of tes[ting.] (space)
> And in the time of oppression he does not abandon her,
>   and does not forget her [in the days of] dread,
>   (6) and in the submission of his soul does not reject [her. (space?)]

Some features of this composition from Cave 4 are immediately apparent. It seems that exactly like the beatitudes in Matthew 5.3–12 there is a set of eight blessings which are then followed by a longer one. In addition to this similarity of form, there are some detailed similarities of content, such as the blessing of those who are 'pure in heart' (Matthew 5.8), though perhaps of even more significance is the way in which both Matthew and Luke have the set of Jesus' beatitudes end with an extended one concerning persecution. In Matthew Jesus speaks of the persecution 'for my sake,' whereas in 4Q525 the persecution is endured for the sake of Wisdom. The significant parallels between 4Q525 and Matthew's beatitudes in particular allow us to conclude that Jesus' teaching was like that of other Jewish wisdom teachers. It is also clear from the comparison of what Jesus had to say with the text from Qumran that his reward clauses provide a distinctive end-time perspective; in several ways Jesus is an eschatological wisdom teacher as his parables of judgment also indicate. Jesus is adapting the content but keeping the form of a traditional teaching pattern.

Jesus is adapting the content but keeping the form of a traditional teaching pattern

Secondly, a nice detail can be seen when a wisdom saying in the non-sectarian *Instruction* (4Q416) is compared with what Jesus teaches. In dealing with practical financial matters the teacher responsible for the composition in the Qumran manuscript very strongly advises his pupils not to try to make money out of what anybody might deposit with them for safe-keeping: 'If someone has left a deposit with you, do not put your hand on it lest it be scorched and your body burnt by its flame; as you have received it, so return it.' Against this Jesus' teaching has an altogether different tone. According to the parable of the talents (Matthew 25.14–30) Jesus requires those with the deposits of others to multiply them assiduously. Though this may be a mere metaphorical expression encouraging listeners to make urgent use of the talents which God has given them, it would seem to make best sense and have all the more force if set alongside other known wisdom teaching. In light of *Instruction* Jesus appears not only be to urging the use of deposited money because of the proximity of divine judgment, but also challenging those who would teach prudence with security. In this case, the difference is as informative for our modern understanding of what Jesus is saying as the similarity is in other instances.

The fresh view which the scrolls provide of Jesus as a Jewish wisdom teacher with end-times concerns can be taken one step further. It is not just a matter of making some comments about what Jesus said, but also of fitting him in to some models so that his role can be understood more clearly. In the non-sectarian *Apocryphon of Levi* (4Q541), Levi seems to provide several descriptions of future priests. In one instance, perhaps a particularly significant eschatological one, the priest is described as providing atonement for all the sons of his generation; despite this, many will despise his wise teaching and his ability to expound matters in parables so that they end up persecuting him vehemently. This pattern of the persecuted wisdom teacher illuminates the combination also to be found in Jesus; many of his Jewish contemporaries would have been readily able to recognize or deny the significance of what he was saying and doing.

5

Conclusion

Beyond Parallelomania

When two phenomena that look alike appear in similar contexts, their relationship to one another needs very careful description and analysis. For historical (most of the scrolls predate Jesus), geographical (Jesus was not active in Judah where most priestly Essenes were), social (Jesus was not part of the priestly establishment), and theological reasons (Jesus taught a view of God's rule that was far more inclusive than the view of the Qumran community) this booklet has argued that Jesus and his followers should be distinguished from the communities

When two phenomena that look alike appear in similar contexts, their relationship needs very careful description and analysis

described in the Dead Sea Scrolls. There is really no place for the straightforward identification of Jesus with the Qumran community.

So how should the many parallels between the two bodies of literature be described? Many more examples of similarities and differences could be given such as in community structure and organization or with regard to attitudes to the law or about Jewish healing practices. Nevertheless, enough has been presented in this booklet to suggest that the scrolls enable the modern reader to appreciate on the one hand many aspects of what was distinctive in Jesus' teaching and in the beliefs of his followers and on the other what was the rehearsing of shared cultural traditions. Part of the chronological and calendrical calculations of the scrolls may lie behind a few of the New Testament traditions. The place of women and how they might function in early Christian communities is surprisingly illuminated from the scrolls. In many places the two bodies of literature contain shared traditions of the interpretation of the Scriptures. The outlines of developing messianic views in the scrolls shed light on the different messianic emphases of the four gospel writers. Wisdom traditions in the Qumran library illuminate the role of Jesus as a particular kind of Jewish wisdom teacher with concerns for the breaking-in of God's rule in the end times.

The scrolls indicate clearly that Jesus was not speaking in a vacuum with sayings that were entirely unique

Altogether the scrolls indicate clearly that Jesus was not speaking in a vacuum with sayings that were entirely unique and so incapable of being grasped. Rather he belonged to the Judaism of his time but combined his insights into God in a highly distinctive manner that eventually led to his death. The way in which his followers experienced his continuing presence amongst them caused them to rework their inherited Jewish tradition afresh as well, in light of his teaching and other activity. The scrolls authenticate and illuminate the Jewishness of Jesus in an unparalleled way and demonstrate intriguingly that, despite their overall concern with Jesus himself, many of the insights of his early Christian followers were continuous with the views of their Jewish contemporaries.

Further Resources

6

A more complete listing of the following guide to resources and further reading on the scrolls is available on the Grove website at www.grovebooks.co.uk

The Dead Sea Scrolls

The Dead Sea Scrolls have virtually all now been published in principal scholarly editions, but there are two handy collections of Hebrew / Aramaic texts with parallel English translations:

- F García Martínez and E J C Tigchelaar, *The Dead Sea Scrolls Study Edition* (Leiden: Brill; Grand Rapids, MI: Eerdmans, 2nd edn, 2000) 2 volumes.

- D W Parry and E Tov (ed), *The Dead Sea Scrolls Reader* (Leiden: Brill, 2003–2005); this has six volumes: 1. Texts Concerned with Religious Law; 2. Exegetical Texts; 3. Parabiblical Texts; 4. Calendrical and Sapiential Texts; 5. Poetic and Liturgical Texts; 6. Additional Genres and Unclassified Texts.

The Scrolls in English translation

G Vermes, *The Complete Dead Sea Scrolls in English* (London: Penguin Books, 5th edn, 1998; now available as a Penguin Classic). This is the best translation with texts in English alone.

General Introductions

J G Campbell, *Deciphering the Dead Sea Scrolls* (Oxford: Blackwell Publishing, 2nd edn, 2003); the best popular introduction which sets the scrolls in a wider historical context.

P R Davies, G J Brooke and P R Callaway, *The Complete World of the Dead Sea Scrolls* (London: Thames and Hudson, 2002); the most lavishly illustrated and wide-ranging introduction.

J C VanderKam and P W Flint, *The Meaning of the Dead Sea Scrolls: Their Significance for Understanding the Bible, Judaism, Jesus, and Christianity*

(San Francisco: HarperSanFrancisco, 2002); particularly good on describing the significance of the scrolls for the better understanding of the history of the transmission of the Old Testament books.

Reference Collection

L H Schiffman and J C VanderKam (eds), *Encyclopedia of the Dead Sea Scrolls* (New York: Oxford University Press, 2000), 2 volumes. Articles on almost everything including the significance of the scrolls for Jesus and for the better understanding of the books of the New Testament.

Website

The website of the Orion Center at the Hebrew University of Jerusalem (http://orion.mscc.huji.ac.il) is the best for a wide range of data and for providing links to others which handle the scrolls responsibly.

The Scrolls and the New Testament

O Betz and R Riesner, *Jesus, Qumran and the Vatican: Clarifications* (London: SCM Press, 1994); the best brief attempt at putting in their place various conspiracy theories and the highly unlikely proposals of B Thiering and R H Eisenman.

J H Charlesworth, (ed), *Jesus and the Dead Sea Scrolls* (New York: Doubleday, 1992); a collection of semi-technical essays on Jesus in light of the scrolls.

C P Thiede, *The Dead Sea Scrolls and the Jewish Origins of Christianity* (Oxford: Lion Publishing, 2000); overstates the case for Cave 7's fragments containing some parts of the New Testament, but with some other useful recent information.